Imaginary Friends

Bluebell Publishing

For Amanda, Karl, Saskia

By the same author:

Poetry

By the Canal (Masque Publishing)
Winter Trees
Cities Like Jerusalem
Homes
The Love Songs of James Dyer
Narratives
Gardening

Plays

Le Conquet (The Refugees)

Short Stories

Aegean Islands

Title page

Nick Monks
Imaginary Friends

Copyright © 2018 by Nick Monks

All rights reserved. No part of this publication may be reproduced, distributed, or transmitted in any form or by any means, including photocopying, recording, or other electronic or mechanical methods, without the prior written permission of the publisher, except in the case of brief quotations embodied in critical reviews and certain other non- commercial uses permitted by copyright law.

**Published September 2018/By Bluebell Publishing
Printed by Lulu**
www.lulu.com

ISBN: 978-0-9955203-5-6

Contents:

Preface

Imaginary Friend 1
Imaginary Friend 2
Imaginary Friend 3
Imaginary Friend 4
Imaginary Friend 5
Imaginary Friend 6
Imaginary Friend 7
Imaginary Friend 8
Imaginary Friend 9
Imaginary Friend 10
Imaginary Enemy 11
Imaginary Friend 12
Imaginary Girlfriend 13
Imaginary Friend 14
Imaginary Friend 15
Imaginary Friend 16
Imaginary Friend 17
Imaginary Friend 18
Imaginary Friend 19
Imaginary Friend 20

Preface

The book was written quickly in two takes. Explores the vicarious phenomena of mind. Which in a world of *ownership* of material objects and *cognitive sciences*, are given less academic attention- to.

The friends are no less real. For not being actual.

Imaginary Friends

Imaginary Friend 1

My friend Darius lies at the bottom,
Of a quarry pool all day
He is an amphibian newt/ frog.
Civil servant and manager and payroll clerk
We cavort in Dorchester, Crewe, Lytham
Beware retirement villages he says
Where I came to as a refugee from a city with no name

He croaks to me. As the sky turns anthracite
Then black then green, then soft plastic
He is similar- to me. Sings Handel's- Water Music song
Also likes Sibelius and George Gershwin
My friend is a silent non- talking friend.
He is not aware of me. Yet though I am not aware of him

Deep like a treasure at the bottom of the quarry pool
All Antediluvian or Cambrian. He croaks
In the time that was before there was this time.

Imaginary Friend 2

My second imaginary friend is a girl with red hair
A bubbly personality. Yet shy and measured in that
While the days oscillate with tarnish and thorny dandelion
She lies deep within, never revealed
A character Moliere forgot to pen
But central to *Le Misanthrope*
Like Livia was central to Rome. Quietly, quietly
Her footsteps on the stair, in the hall. Never heard.

Imaginary Friend 3

My third imaginary friend comes in the dead of night
I keep her like a winged waterfall catching vase
We cavorted in some dead divine city
Until in the ruins of Rome
After the barbarians
She comes bearing fruits and cashew nuts
Me handcuffed and shackled to a Victorian radiator
She moves like whispers
I never move one iota. My cataract eyes fixed on the
Leaning keeled overladen bookcase.

Imaginary Friend 4

My forth imaginary friend is a real friend
Who I never see. So- they can be a facet of imagination
He is a date in the diary in thirty weeks- time
As the year marches across the terrible high nettles
The deep mud of the land they have not got- round to
building on
An e mail address that will reply aptly
A voice mail replied to within one hour.

Imaginary Friend 5

My fifth imaginary friend is Rhiannon a Welsh Goddess
She tarries at the bridge over the River Ribble
Sometimes she stays for hours. Appears in milliseconds
Then an unannounced departure
She has raven black hair and is eternal
Moving in a different dimension. She is a gift bestowed
Her mortal world was forest clearing hamlet. She visits me
On- housing estate and intwixt city skyline.

Imaginary Friend 6

My sixth imaginary friend is Lawrence Durrell
He like me is allured by Ionian and Aegean Sea
Citrus and olive tree scent.
The music of Mediterranean waves
He is an inventive and bumptious character
Who escaped the bleak towns of England
He is over there on Corfu, guiding with a cold drink, my
over here-ness in Preston.

He pens poems of green sea horses. Tide oscillated
While Aegean kelp sways. And an ancient ship heads for
Heraklion.

Imaginary Friend 7

When the night becomes. From the forest
Were now there are flat rapeseed fields
A man in purple shawl. Beckons and asks me to write poems
He is the nameless ancestor, in the disappeared forest
We each know the route the terrain. He leaves me
Untouched, like moors stream water
We share the nightjar, the nightingale, the rose hips, the wild strawberry.

Imaginary Friend 8

I lost Denise in a snow storm on the Salisbury plain
I lost John my neighbour, in getting in a removals van lorry cab
As I walk through Preston city centre. Thousands of Brexit British burp and scowl
In between I think I see each of them in aged faces
As the helicopter whirrs overhead, and cars pass over the ornate road
My lost dissidents appear. No amount of retrospect can
Change seeing them. Even though they could be any
Anonymous passer-by.

Imaginary Friend 9

My eighth imaginary friend resides in a cottage
In a valley of the West Sussex downs.
She wears becomingly light floral dresses
Of which the hems scrape pollen from the night meadows
We are writing a thesis on snow together
And differentiate from the maddened-
Twisted crowds of Constantinople
Hurriedly colleting possessions, as Sultan Mehmed
Pulls the ships ashore.

Imaginary Friend 10

My tenth imaginary friend isn't born yet
But reads my poetic dirges in 3010. Opens and closes
The case with the brass watch Frank got-
For fifty years working in a cotton mill
She walks across the lunar surface of Preston
With concerns of the "Age of Questions"
With her imaginary and real friends and taps the postcode
Into- a people carrying drone.

Imaginary Enemy 11

My imaginary enemy has come from the Nordic
I hide with my retinue in the swamps and
Marshes of Somerset
I desire to build a kingdom of on Christianity
When I had defeated my imaginary enemy- Guthrum
At the battle of Edington
I let the Vikings stay and marry and work.
And became King Alfred in Londinium- a kingdom.

Imaginary Friend 12

My twelfth imaginary friend rejected
The middle- class world of professions
He was brought up in
And sits on a Havana veranda sipping gin and lime
Reading the daily local English papers
To write novels on Cuba/Mexico/Sierra Leone/ Congo
Basin/British Cameroons/Haiti
As he spends most of his time away, I never see him.

Imaginary Girlfriend 13

My imaginary girlfriend lives in a tent in the ruins of a
war- torn country
She does not know me
And comes across the forests and mountains in search of
Doc leaf and clover flower
It is impossible we will ever meet. Thus- we are together
eternally
As a possibility that is infinitely open. Pure and untainted.

Imaginary Friend 14

My imaginary friend is directing her armies across Europe
She comes from broken families
She chases a dream
That will turn inward and be destroyed
With the rise of a new kingdom and era
She is tantamount to empress/ prostitute/ tramp.

Imaginary Friend 15

My fourteenth imaginary friend is Tiresias
A blind prophet of Apollo,
Who was transformed into a woman for seven years
He spanned seven generations in Thebes
And is clairvoyant
He is the son of the shepherd Everes
And the nymph Chariclo
As he is blind he can never see me with eyes vision
As he existed in ancient Greece, he is also-
Of a different era.

Imaginary Friend 16

My sixteenth imaginary friend must remain hidden like a dot so small
Non- can see the telephone calls, the e mails, the lines from me to her
The footprints from house to house, in the snow
If she can remain hidden. Then she will remain an imaginary friend.

Imaginary Friend 17

My seventeenth imaginary friend left her husband.
Drank vodka for five days
Slept around. Then she married a woman footballer
She has rightly outflanked guilt utterly. And comes by
Trumpet blast announcements
Into the monastery, nunnery, court room, conference
Centre, she rejuvenates and binds wounds.

Imaginary Friend 18

My eighteenth imaginary friend sits in an
Office of a sock making/ sewing shop
He is rude and incendiary
I leave him behind and ignored as I travel in the quiet
Room over all the universe
Him griping in the sepia hollows of a room, with a dim low
Voltage electric bulb.

Imaginary Friend 19

My nineteenth imaginary friend lives in an office room of a bank
They put a bed out for her when the bank closes
I met her once upon a time to discuss overdrafts and bank charges
She holds a thread of meetings, I hold a thread of meetings
Unconventional, we changed the topic one day, and fled to Venezuela leaving a goodbye note, and house keys.

Imaginary Friend 20

My twentieth imaginary friend is a mermaid
In the Irish sea
She combs her hair on serpentine rocks
Then dives into the elements of salt water away
Into the Atlantic. And I follow leaving a dishevelled bed.
A locked door. A thousand unsent letters. A broken clock.

Nick Monks lives in Preston, Lancashire, UK. He studied Philosophy at Hull University. Worked and travelled around the world for about seven years.

He has published 7 poetry collections. Had many poems in poetry magazines. Worked in scores of jobs. Is currently trying to write a novel.

A copy of this book is held at The National Poetry Library, London. The British Library, London. The Bodleian Libraries of the University of Oxford. Cambridge University Library. The National Library of Scotland. The Library of Trinity College Dublin. The National Library of Wales.

www.ingramcontent.com/pod-product-compliance
Lightning Source LLC
Chambersburg PA
CBHW031440040426
42444CB00006B/899